# EXPRESSIONS

## Eleanor on Her Life

Photographed and Edited by
**A. E. Woolley**

# Dedicated to Pat and Beverly

A special appreciation to Fred Brown, Patricia
Robinson, Beverly and Duke Janda and Al Garrett
for their unshakable faith.

## Other books by A. E. Woolley, PhD

Persia/Iran: A Pictorial Treasury of 25 Centuries
Images of South Africa
Two Under The Eagle
Photography: A Practical and Creative Introduction
Creative 35mm Techniques
Camera Journalism
Night Photography
Photographic Lighting
Traveling With Your Camera

ISBN 0-918513-00-6

Manufactured in the United States of America.
Typesetting by Perfect Printing.
Printing by Science Press.

Copyright 1984 A. E. Woolley, PhD
Published by Woolley Publications, Inc.
Cherry Hill, New Jersey 08034

# Table of Contents

**S**ilence settled into the room.

The lady walked to center stage. She carried no baton. She did not turn her back to the audience, rather she faced the expectant faces. As she lifted her hands in greeting, the silence ceased and a roar of affection filled the hall. Mrs. Eleanor Roosevelt motioned for quiet with her hands. She commanded her listeners with the same delicate sensitivity one expects from a concert conductor. And once again Mrs. Roosevelt expressed her feelings and opinions on a wide range of subjects, including but not limited to, politics, world conditions, racial problems, women's rights, self-image or worth and her husband. She postulated the attention of her audience, punctuating her message with fluidity of her hands; an extension of her words.

Eleanor Roosevelt's expressive hands questured, accentuated, emphasized, punctuated and directed her audiences. She commanded her listener. No conductor ever possessed a greater collation of communication signals.

Mrs. Roosevelt, one of the world's most articulate women, enjoyed respect for her views on politics, racial problems and domestic as well as foreign situations. She suffered personal scars from constant criticism because she advocated ideas and practices well ahead of the accepted mores of her time, whether the issues were social, racial or political.

In her final years, she devoted much of her time to helping nations and individuals identify problems; and search for solutions. Her goal seemed always to achieve more understanding between people and nations.

Whether in casual discussions or forum speaking, Eleanor Roosevelt used her hands for audience attention, kept rhythm and tempo with the words she used and accentuated her points bringing her listeners into her attitude whether they agreed or not.

Her words stated her case. Her hands and gestures expressed her sounds.

On October 11, 1984, the world will honor Eleanor Roosevelt's 100th birthday. No other American woman has enjoyed the respect reserved for this lady. Not only did she serve her nation with dignity during her First Lady years, but she went on to rise to even greater heights on her own merit. With the foundation laid over two decades, she chose to render a supporting role to the man she married, and the man whom she no longer loved. The pain of knowing she had been betrayed lasted even to the day Franklin D. Roosevelt died. The other woman who had wedged between Franklin and Eleanor visited the dying president the week of his death. Yet, the pain seemed to temper Eleanor Roosevelt, who would elevate to a position of world importance that only her husband would have rivaled in the post World War II years.

I consider the brief time I knew Eleanor Roosevelt a great privilege. The photographs that fill this book are the product of several occasions (the last being her 75th birthday) when she spoke to audiences at the State University of New York where I served as a professor. Most of the pictures never have been published before. Perhaps in their virgin appearance herein, they are a birthday present to the world.

A.E. Woolley, PhD
Cherry Hill, NJ

"**W**hen I feel right in what I do, I cannot afford, as a self-respecting individual, to refuse to do a thing merely because it will make me disliked, or bring down a storm of criticism on my head."

"Our obligation to the world is our obligation to our own future."

"The refugees of the world are a constant and painful reminder of the breakdown of civilization through the stupidity of war. They are the permanent victims."

"For the first time in my life, I can say just what I want. It is wonderful to feel free."

"In a free country, a free press can say whatever it chooses. While I did have to put up with indignities from certain quarters, I can say that in the long run it does not matter. It is what one does that determines people's final judgements."

ON FREEDOM

"I remember little of what my husband did in the legislature except that he came out for women's suffrage. I was shocked. I had never given the question serious thought. I took it for granted that men were superior creatures and knew more about politics than women did, and while I realized that if my husband were a suffragist I probably must be too, I cannot claim to have been a feminist in those early days."

"My grandmother had taught me that a woman's place was not in the public eye, and the idea clung to me through all the Washington years."

"Ever since World War I my interest had been in doing real work, not in being a dilettante."

"My lecture trips gave me more money for things I wanted to do than my husband could afford to give me."

# ON WOMEN'S RIGHTS

"It takes

courage

to love."

"By earning my own money, I had recently enjoyed a certain amount of financial independence and had been able to do things in which I was personally interested."

"At the time I married, my income varied from $5,000 to $8,000 a year."

"Young women with a good education find it impossible to become just housewives and mothers. They need outside interests."

14

# ON SELF-IMAGE

"I was always afraid of something; of the dark, of displeasing people, of failure. Anything I accomplished had to be done across a barrier of fear."

"I'd like some good, straight teeth to give me a better looking mouth."

"I had only three assets. I was keenly interested, I accepted every challenge and opportunity to learn more, and I had great energy and self-discipline."

"If you gain in knowledge and experience, new opportunities open up for you."

"My chief objective, as a girl, was to do my duty. Not my duty as I saw it, but as laid down for me by other people. It never occured to me to revolt."

"gratitude and love are not to be had for the asking; they are not to be bought. They are not for sale."

"I was beginning to make occasional speeches. On occasions Louis Howe went with me, sat in the back of the audience and gave me pointers for improvement. His advice was: Have something you want to say, say it and sit down."

"It was not until middle age that I had the courage to develop interests of my own."

"It seemed stupid to have the gift of life and not use it to the utmost of one's ability."

**"I** did not want my husband to be president. I never realized however, that it was impossible to keep a man out of public service when that was what he wanted and was undoubtedly well equipped for."

"My love for Franklin died long ago, but by believing in his objectives I rendered him a service of love."

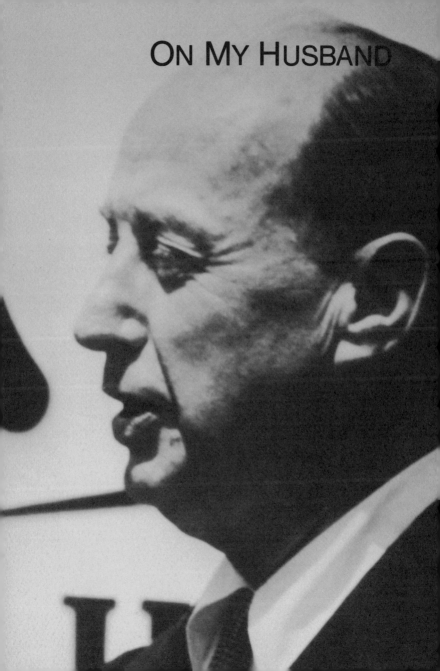

ON MY HUSBAND

**M**y husband and I agreed that we would put an equal amount into the house account, and we lived easily and comfortably, if not luxuriously, on $600 a month."

"My husband asked me to take over the inspection of the institutions. I learned to look into pots on the stove and to find out if the contents corresponded to the menu."

"I never knew a man who gave me a greater sense of security. I never knew him to face life or any problem that came up with fear."

"I've grown more patient with age and have learned from my husband that no leader can be too far ahead of his followers."

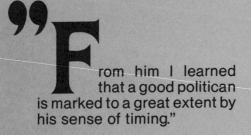

"**F**rom him I learned that a good politican is marked to a great extent by his sense of timing."

"I should have tried much harder to help him through this awful war. I used to pray every night that he would be spared to carry on, but he did not know that. He did so much want to see a good peace."

"I have the memory of an elephant. I can forgive, but I cannot forget."

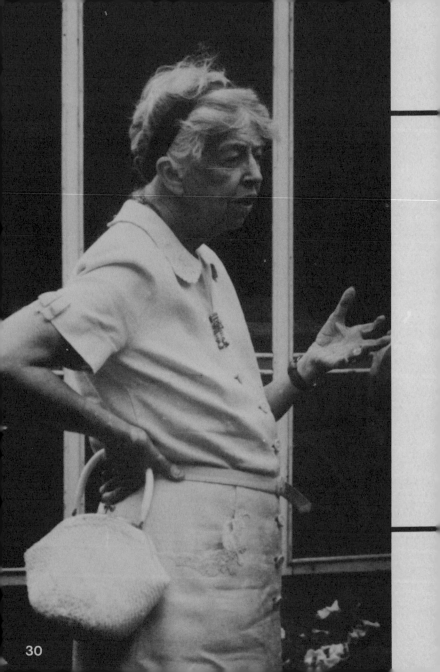

"There is a big muddled world with so much to be done. We must think of hunger not as an abstraction but as an empty stomach, learn to care, increase our understanding, and have an hospitable mind which is open like a window to currents of light and air from all sides."

"Among our best workers in all campaigns are the women. They will do the dull work and fill the uninteresting speaking engagements which none of the men are willing to undertake."

"I thought, and still think, that a good business executive does not make a good government administrator, nor does an administration of businessmen make for good government."

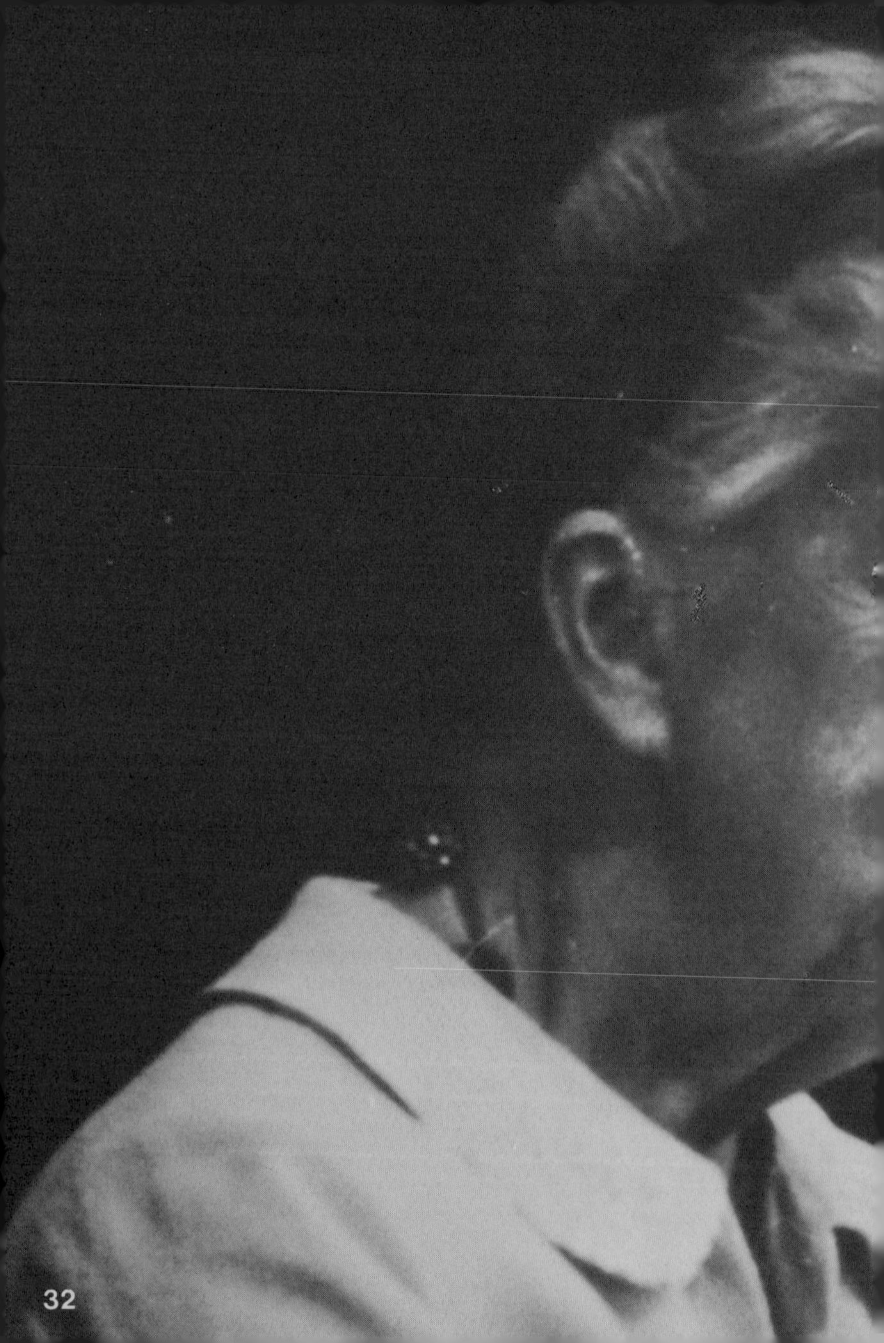

"**A**s I've grown older, my personal objectives have long since blended into my public objectives."

"This idea may seem preposterous, but in political life you grow suspicious. The strategists on both sides weight how far they can go without awakening in the people a feeling that the rules of fair play have not been observed."

"It takes the slow evolution of years to bring about change."

"Unless our citizenship is constantly improving, our natural resources will be of little value."

"People who feel intensely inspire action in others."

"A majority may be temporarily wrong, but a majority that remained over a period of years was usually right."

**Y**ou can accomplish a great deal more if you care deeply about what is happening to other people rather than saying in apathy or discouragement, "Oh, what can I do? What use is one person? I might as well not bother."

"More and more people are coming to realize what affects an individual affects mankind."

"We must have freedom and decency among nations to have peace."

"I wonder if young people realize that every new form of government — fascism, communism, democracy — had for its purpose the making of a world in which people could be content and happy?"

"There are three fundamentals for human happiness — work, love and faith. These must be made possible for all, men and women alike."

ON WORLD CONDITIONS

# ON CIVIL RIGHTS

"One is not asking for equal rights, but equal opportunities. When opportunities are obtainable, the rights will take care of themselves."

"Sooner or later a nation has to make up its mind to be united, or fall apart."

"Sometimes I think we're a little too calm when we encounter prejudice."

"If we're not going to be able to have ordinary contacts with people who are citizens of our own country, how can we expect to have the same kind of contacts with people who live in different parts of the world?"

"What a man can earn has no relationship whatsoever to his capacity or his worth as an individual."

**W**hen changes need to be brought about in politics, we must count on the youth, since their elders have grown accustomed to set practices."

"More people are ruined by victory than by defeat."

"All of us have an obligation to live together peacefully."

"The need of a symbol is a very deep need in human nature."

# Personal and Political Highlights

1884    October 11, birth of Anna Eleanor Roosevelt
1892    Mother died, lived with maternal grandmother, Mrs. Valentine G. Hall
1899    Lived and educated in England, three years
1905    Married Franklin D. Roosevelt
1911    FDR elected to New York State Senate
1913    FDR appointed Assistant Secretary of the Navy, moved to Washington, DC
1920    Enrolled in secretarial skills school
1920    FDR defeated for Vice President
1921    Joined Board of League of Women Voters
1924    Finance Chairman, New York Democratic Party
1925    Founded Val-Kill Furniture Shop, Hyde Park
1927    Bought, and taught at, Todhunter School
1928    FDR elected Governor of New York
1932    FDR elected President of United States
1932    First Lady for 12 years, to 1945
1936    Began "My Day" newspaper column
1941    Assistant Director, Office of Civilian Defense
1945    FDR died; moved to Hyde Park, New York
1945    Appointed a delegate to United Nations by President Harry S. Truman
1947    Elected Chairman of Commission on Human Rights, United Nations
1962    Death at age 78